Letters to Life

NEHA BHAGAT SANGAR

BlueRoseONE.com
Stories Matter

First Published in May 2022

ISBN: 978-93-5611-353-4

BLUEROSE PUBLISHERS
www.bluerosepublishers.com
info@bluerosepublishers.com
+91 8882 898 898

Cover Design:
Geetika Kandari

Typographic Design:
Pooja Sharma

Distributed by: BlueRose, Amazon, Flipkart

Dedication

I dedicate this book to my father for bestowing upon me the zest and fire to lead a spiritual life and for giving me a life standard to strive for.

To my Guru Sri Sri Ravi Shankar Ji for choosing me as a part of his vision to seek the truth. I am forever grateful to him for lifetimes.

To my mother, for being my pillar, my angel, the Iron lady of my life. My first Guru since I was born.

To my dear husband for loving me unconditionally and being a true driver for me to achieve higher.

To my sisters for being my life support system and inspiring me to be righteous and great.

To my friends and all the beautiful souls I have met who have bewildered me with their innocence and dedication as a seeker of truth.

Foreword

What you hold in your hands dear readers is a dream. Not just of the author, Neha Bhagat's, but also one of millions other who aspire to etch their feelings in a book.

The words may be hers, but the thoughts are universal. More than once you will find yourselves touching unknown depths of your souls. You will be sometimes thrown and rocked, while at other times cradled by the waves of her poetry.

Neha has many times been my guide in life, bestowed with a depth of character and wisdom that betrays her age. Yet she still has the childlike innocence that is all but lost in society today.

It is an honour to introduce her first book. She has indeed very bravely bared her soul. It is a rendition of life in love and pain. Lose yourself.

Suveera Sharma
Columnist, Blogger

Acknowledgements

I would like to acknowledge great support from my husband 'Varun Sangar' for encouraging me in every way to publish this book, his life as an army officer and his unconditional love has inspired me in many ways to seek the truth.

I would like to thank my father ' L.K. Sharma' for being him, as I have inherited a spirit of enquiry towards the soul from him.

I would like to thank my Guru 'Sri Sri Ravi Shankar Ji' for his grace upon me I owe my wisdom and light to him.

Last but not the least I would like to thank Blue Rose publishers for helping me realize my dream of being a writer.

Preface

How would you feel if you lived in a land of love, peace and joy where every breath was full of excitement to live the next moment, where you feel so secure knowing that god is your own friend. Life moves on and you get lured partly by your desires and partly by the so called sanity of life, you get driven away from that land to a conditioned "real" world. And now you are stuck.

Living each day looking for trails and messages from that heaven like land. Coiled by worldly responsibilities and duties you feel incomplete and broken; not knowing when and how you would have that union again.

Thus, this book was born to me. My soul struggling sometimes enjoying the confined boundaries of a homely life seeing it as gift from god himself and sometimes longing to be back to that land.

In these spells of love and pain, in these moments of inner calling versus the inherent need for domestication these are some letters that I have written to life through which I pray each reader connects to their own self and be one with my thoughts.

Contents

She

Sometimes when the night is silent and free
I sit to write a glorious story.
A story of dreams that never found their shore,
of valour and grit in her smile that she wore.

A tireless mother,
a selfless wife,
an angelic daughter,
and so much more.

How magically she belonged to herself very few know,
she was her charm,
her own weapon.
In this world of fake
she was a rare gem.

This is the story of that untold 'She',
a story of you, a story of me.

Standing strong facing all the judgements and bickery
I call you to, break free!

The length of your skirts
your uncultured child,
too beautiful, too less, outspoken or too wild?

Break through the cocoon
like a revolutionary butterfly
I see your soul, it's time to fly.

But today if you wonder how far you have reached?
which glories you touched?
and which ones did you just preach?
You will find your god stare at your shine from above
through the gentle breeze he would whisper in your ears:

"The depth of your smile is a measure of your success my
love
The depth of your smile is a measure of your success my
love"

I die everyday

I die every day
deaf to my inner voice,
incapable of mending my ways.
With every changing drama of this life I sway,
I die every day!

That beauty that truth I know of
I am unable to seek it feels far away.
I die every day.

In every ego that I win,
with every dream that I overlooked with laze,
I die every day.

To live the madness of passion,
to die for it if I may.
All the sweet glories and comfort feels bitter today.

A space un done, so empty in my heart lay,
I died today.
I die every day!

To the Forests

To the forests
I write a letter to thee,
in love in pain
I cry in apology.

So beautiful pure wild you sway
a sacred arrangement of god's play.
I listen to you of our ungrateful ways,
unworthy of your grace we fail.

But now and then
I seek you in sweet solitude,
for a union of me with myself
that peaceful embrace.
You awaken in me a blessed joy,
that truth, stillness and extreme wilderness.

And as I rest on your roots dear tree,
this ancient love story of you and me.
What draws me to you I do not know,
I feel your earth inside me
like an old saint you whisper to me 'Just Be'.

Your birds, your flowers, your mountains
your ants, your fruits, and rivers too.
Engaged in sacred divine duty,
so silent, lawful and mighty!

Dear forests,
I owe my soul to thee.
As my god pulsates through the life in your beings,
we rip away your beauty and your fruits.
Silently you give
yet watchful of our sins.
How long will you continue to forgive?

To, the forests
so great, dark and deep.
I share your pain

I owe my soul to thee.

I write to you

And cry in apology.

Meditation to the soul

Just as what
breath is to life,
water is to thirst,
food is to hunger,
and love is to a blunder.

Just as what
a mother is to her child,
that innocence of the wild.
What freedom means to the caged,
the wisdom of the ancient and aged.

That adventure ever new untold,
the highest beauty to behold,
It excites, belongs to the bold.

That is what meditation is to the soul.
my limitless whole !
That is what
meditation is to the soul.

The World ends in me

The world and all its experiences end inside me.
Each as a feeling inside that I see,
giving me the power of choice to be,
what I want to be.
That's the Power in me,
I can choose how I feel
and be what I want to be.

The Martyr

As he took his last breath in haste,

his blood it spilled to make the earth a purer place.

The air got gripped in a cold grief

with a higher pride it now blows free.

Listen, it whispers to you his valorous story

a real life hero, a martyr is he!

Conquering the highest fear,

his land, his first love.

Thud ! Boom ! those gunshot sounds his ears are now numb,

his wounds now bleed, they mark his bravery.

A hero, a martyr is he!

But as he lay dead there.
He makes the gods cry.
They sing songs of his courage,
with all the unanswered whys.
But Immortal he is, there are no goodbyes,
A martyr he is, forever Alive!

Take it slow

My life is one moment
the more I break it
the more it grows.
Peace and abundance flows
and I let it flood my soul
with all the life it beholds.
And I remind myself:
'take it slow
take it slow'!

That small miniscule of time,
the smaller you break it
the more subtle it goes.
A deep mystery unfolds,
take it slow!

That pretty smile on her face,
an adventure untold.
Hear it, rejoice it,
let it flood your soul.
Embrace the love that flows
take it slow.

The power of a still mind
unhurried unrushed for the 'gold'.
These are precious treasures to find,
moment by moment, calm and cantered
breathe in the beauty it holds.
Take it slow!

God lies in the small things
the finer you go,
more power unfolds.
Take it slow!

That warm ray that shines in your face.
and the cool breeze that blows.
That cold rain drop which tickled your soul.
be busy in living their joy,
in these small wonders
the divine unfolds.
Take it slow!

So Divine

When god decided to manifest ancient sacred wisdom,
a medium for his of love to shine.
Born today with glory and greatness,
is someone so divine!

His aura demands natural respect.
He received many salutes from the highest shrines.
Yet he stays humble and silent,
like the depth of an ocean that he holds inside.
The epitome of righteousness, truth and values so fine.
Born today is someone so divine!

Don't mistake his sometimes hard exterior,
it's just to keep safe all that beauty inside.
It takes efforts to hold all that sacredness
that can make a million shine.
Born today is someone so divine.

My father he is and blessed I am
I thank god and fold my hands.
Worthy enough, to be born to him,
earning those blessed karmas and sins.
As I receive and contain a small part of his wisdom
it is enough to make my whole life shine.
My father he is unbelievably mine,
Born today is someone so divine.

Every time you come and go

My room is now silent I feel a strange lack
your clothes are all gone and packed.
Your fragrance, it slowly fades away from the air
but why in my breath I can smell you there?
My mind is so full and teases me like a foe
tiredly I begin my journey,
Why do I feel a little low?
Every time you come and go.

I happily lose my promises and all the precious goals,
for when you are here,
there is no merrier joy to follow.
Every time you come and go

Your presence heals,
your absence makes me longing for more.
Trying to get used to this comfort and pain duo
Every time you come and go.

That child in me that you awaken
I heavily get back to being mature,
I embrace my duties they keep me busy

help me bank myself to the shore.
Every time you come and go.

Wish I could lock my joy inside
wish that time with you I could rewind.
But days pass on, the goals are reset
and life stage is set for more fake shows.
Every time you come and go

The clock ticks away.
your service to the nation!
Your duty calls,
my head over my heart
I wake you up "get ready love, you have to go"

We are mere puppets and he is the charmer.
Oh it kills me a little did you know?
every time you come and go

Let's keep moving on,
we will meet again
time waits for none
I am so glad it doesn't.

As I wait gleefully to see u again
the date nears the joy grows.
Every time you come and go

Yes you leave me so full, so empty and low
Every time you come and go.

My Inner Self

I know
I love, I care
nothing to loose,
Nothing to dare.

Like ripples on water
disturb its calmness,
my deep beautiful sea
is in despair.

When I lose all that I am not
these impure feelings and thoughts,
What is that 'I' that stares?

Settled in my self
pure, beautiful, Innocent,
powerful and fair.

Come settle in me
my 'self' cries.
An ancient love,
the sacred union of me with myself.
It's the only truth amongst these lies.

Like Ripples in the sea
are a part of the sea.
Like clouds that vanish
and leave behind the sky.
I want to be one with thee.

So calm, pure, powerful and beautiful
neither empty nor full.

That which is found in loosing oneself.
That which is the background
beyond, life pain and breath.

So easy it is, that it is toughest to find
my inner self
It is that love divine!

The hug of a tree

Grow a tree, hug it and sway.
Play with a child flow in her smiles.
Follow that ant see where it goes,
that joyful bird which hops on the tree,
go on adore its show.

Incomplete unaware undone and rough.
Our soul is calling
it can't be so tough.

The trees and you. the birds and you,
the ants, the leaves, and the flowers too.
They are connected to that smile in you.
That peace they give,
is overlooked in the haste.
But you be fast and busy
there is no time to waste.

Oh! what a waste this life would be
so blind and moulded
that the real beauty we unsee.
The little things bring great joy
the bigger jewels take you by.

That tree you hug, will hug you back,
that flower will bloom, sit for a while.
There is no purpose, no lists to complete,
when empty the real journey begins,
drop the efforts
Just be!
Feel the hug of that tree.

The Wanderer

Like a speck of dust
when the winds are wild
sways here and there
in directions undefined.

Helpless and tired,
amused and forgotten,
consumed in fakeness,
in empty self-gratifications
it yearns for its ground.

My mind is such
looking for its home
attracted by fake promises
of empty joys it doesn't know.
It's so tired and away
should find it's home.

This world is miraculous
endless pleasures and emotions
that beckon us so often.
Those colours and tastes,

positions and expectations
beauty and fame,
images and names,
and tiring mind games.

Such are it's seekings
that leave it empty
It is such a fool
as nothing remains
as if water was strained.

Go look for your home,
I awaken my mind
go find your purpose
let it shine.

There is a life

It's beautiful and content
an effortless journey
with peace and rest.
Settle In that peace
I tell it to ease.

Possess it and let it grow
this world is but an empty show
and empty fake show!

Real life Hero

I write this for you
yes you reading this out there
I write this for you I hope you stay.
Isn't it just another of yours happy pleasant days?
Wake up to a story I invite you to today,
a story of feelings, sacrifice, and of brave ways.
It has a hero who loves to dare
he is your own, a hero of yours
By now you are curious
so let me share more.

An ordinary man
with an extraordinary life
his life is tough and glorious.
Be it the seas, mountains or plains
Freezing temperatures or the scorching sun's pain.
He lives in tough terrains.

Not for himself, neither for fame
nor for money, but for you,
he smiles away the pain.
Yeah he does it for you

Let it not go in vain.

He stays away from his family,
his beautiful wife,
As his little child drifts into the sleepy night,
he sleeps far from him restless
not knowing if the next sun will see him alive.
He can charm any lady
with his chivalrous ways.
A complete gentleman
you will fall for his gaze.
If you have one
keep him safe!

Those loud gun shots, his ears are numb.
The taste of his mother's food he has not forgotten.
That arm there bleeds it's a sweet pain
it's a mark of his valour
and most welcome!

Oh isn't he a hero
A real hero he is!
He happily dies for your safety
does God have a greater responsibility?

All the movies out there

and the theatres show,

give you a perfect image of a hero.

These heroes dance, look good in fake loves

we pay them money

and fill them in our hearts.

While this real life hero

he dies a death to a godly birth.

With his death...

dies your shame!

Yes his death there makes you inhumane.

So let's know our real life heroes

and the glory of their lives.

Let's know their names
it's our duty to keep them alive.

They show a life that we should strive.
salute them much and pay your respect.
As a stranger's life is what they protect.

Let it flow

That space when the mind is still
and the heart surrenders to his will.

No effort to live, thinks, or exist.
I relax in that space,
I belong there.
No doer-ship
it's beyond our ways.

Where I cease
and isness flows.
The more I die
the more it unfolds.

In that space let me live
let me grow
let it be
let it flow.

There lies a truth so deep, so vast.

I can't escape

I want it to last.

In that space let me live,

let me grow,

let it be

let it flow!

Beautiful Inside

Our lives are fast, our ways are rich.
Beauty can be bought
self images can be created.
Days pass on, we live so busy
to stop time! breathe, it's not easy.
Beauty and looks are so important,
simplicity and purity are ancient.
But what is beauty in its truest sense
I question myself.

I know a girl, so simple and pure.
She lives peacefully, gracefully flows.
Loves her work is sincere to the core
She is cheerful has a happy glow
Has no sense of fashion
Never did it lure!

Her face is quiet a calmness prevails
proudly she follows her heart's trails.
Often some bliss teases her days
It makes her joyful like a little girls play.
But underneath this joy there is a calling so deep

It's new, wonderful, yet doesn't let her sleep.

There lies her journey so unknown and meaningful

She is excited, Its soulful

She secretly cherishes this beauty so deep

I question myself this is my revenge

What is Beauty in its truest sense?

A heart that gives, a soul that lives.

Daring to live to the heart's desire

brings ageless beauty

It's a burning fire.

Sharing and caring in love is the drug.

Wouldn't your cheeks blush from the warmth of that hug?

Our talents that we offer to others

leaves us with a sweet fragrance that no perfume can gather.

Beauty is important

but the job begins inside.

There are some un pretty faces with the most comforting smiles.

Pretty people can be seen everywhere,

but to have a beautiful heart that's rare.

So let's decorate our inner soul

and be a living proof of God's work.

As this 'beauty' it's an inside goal.

My mind is my own foe

Where there is no you
and the descriptions end.
A space so free in nothingness
As the mind ceases
where do all the questions end ?
what do we achieve, when we stop the goals
where existence is not an effort!

What is the reason of this separation?
Who am I, If I am you
Who are you if all is sublime?

Like bubbles rising in water, know not their existence
Let me settle in that calmness behind,
let me settle in that peace undefined.
The more I describe it the farther I go
My mind is my foe
my mind is my own foe.

How deep did it remain?

Can you drop the comforts,
fire that spark for the light within?
Can you face your fears and run in that rain,
Or does it sound in vain?

How far can you go for that love?
That journey so hazy
you have been so lazy.
There is no greater pain.
How far did you go for your love
how deep did it remain?

Ur endless smile that ached
that peace was beyond all gains.
How far did u go for that love?
How deep did it remain?

The gods delight in the song you sang
that love so deep until only love remains.
Where there is no two
but just longing and fulfilment.

That divine carefree dance
of shame and shamelessness
of a sweet madness
How deep it remain?
Did you lose it
in the fake worldly love and pain.
Did it all go in vain?
sheltered from the world's sanity!
And I ask again
how far can you go for that love?
how deep did it remain?

That undying love
unconditional beyond the mind.
Comforting and secure
more beautiful than beauty itself.
How deep did it remain?
How deep did it remain?

With Love

Today as I stare at life's trials,
those huge mountains to conquer
make me sigh!

And a voice inside
begins to go high.

That bud is in slumber
let those petals unfold
let your colours, fragrances
add beauty to the world.

Kill that devil, strong as rusted iron
with the heat of self-love.

Let the air intoxicate you,
with the melody of
comfort and contentment
of courage and will.

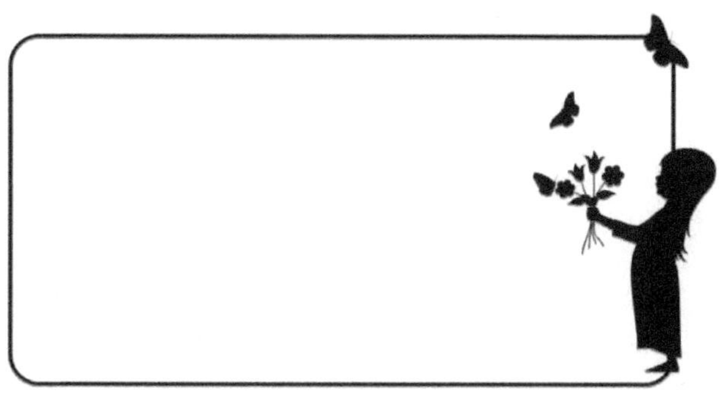

That secret victory
shining in your smile
Let it sparkle in others joy.

Ring that bell,
raise every flag,
reach the end,
watch gods celebrate
In your victory's delight!

Sacrifice!
rejoice the nectar of a committed soul
Where every action is an offering
to that sacred goal!

With love,

embrace it,

for you are the best dare

for which you will ever die for

with love.

A Note to the Reader

Dear Reader,

I feel honoured that my thoughts could reach you.

That in this world full of intellect and judgement my nascent yet innocent words could enter your mind and heart.

I believe that some journeys are so sacred that they begin when the deep realms of the heart are knocked.

In the journey of my life, if you would like to reach out to me in any way, I can be contacted at

Gmail: Nehabhagatsangar@gmail.com

Instagram: @neha.bhagat.3158

I feel deeply grateful that our paths have crossed in a humble yet significant way.

Thanking you,

Neha